Prayers, Supplications, and Intercessions

Latoera O'Neal

ISBN 978-1-64028-206-3 (Paperback)
ISBN 978-1-64028-207-0 (Digital)

Christian Faith Publishing, Inc.
296 Chestnut Street
Meadville, PA 16335
www.christianfaithpublishing.com

Printed in the United States of America

To every soul that is overshadowed by our fallen nature

in reference to false belief systems, lies, abuses,
hardships, shortcomings (whatever the case),
insecurities, adversities, and/or calamities

due to our own personal disconnection from daily
fellowship in communion with our Holy
God and His word: the Gospel of Jesus Christ.

Amen.

Contents

Believe

Don't Judge Me

DON'T JUDGE ME but love me
when I've fallen, minister.
Restore me in meekness unless you also be tempted

There is no sin uncommon to man; we are equal
So DON'T JUDGE ME
Be the example and teach me;
condemnation should never reach me
now that I'm in Christ Jesus.
A new creature old things are passed.
I am new, so
DON'T JUDGE ME.

As I die daily, encourage and uplift me;
stop speaking against me; weapons formed
MISS ME!

The King is listening,
binding, rebuking hindrances;
mind transformed, complete deliverance,
free from the deeds of the enemy.

DON'T JUDGE ME!

I know you see me;
fortified city, victory breathing, scripture gleaning:
Power of God … Seasoned!

Warring and interceding, uprooting mountains,
and people still not believing
the evidence of King Jesus

Blinded by false belief systems,
religious doctrines, brimstone and fire messages;
Judgement Day has not come
So don't judge before it's time
Let God finish his work in me which he has begun

DON'T JUDGE ME!

A Thought

To encourage in love
produces fruits of prosperity
Money, success, achievements
run out.

Character, integrity, faithfulness, and love
can never fail
They speak volumes to multitudes
even when no one is listening

Provider

I'm nauseous; my spirit is stirred up.
I'm hyped, overexcited,
so happy, I begin crying.

The lies are all behind me.
I stand on the truth; I walk with word.
I live by faith. I sleep with grace,
wake up to mercy,
never hungered, never thirsty.

I partook and tasted now, I can never turn away from it!
It's my lifestyle
to remain in this relationship.
I got to be faithful
when I fall short.
Lord, please be patient.
Teach me.

I'm wrong; correct me.
You've already invested time,
good work, and some light.

And I know you won't deny.
The Good Shepherd, come get your sheep that went astray.

God's Righteousness Lives

Lord,
How can one born in sin be right?
How can one expect righteousness when made from sin?
Yes, I have the spirit, the breath in my nostril;
the spirit is willing but the flesh is weak

So disobedient, so rebellious to things pertaining to the spirit
This is my truth; my life has revealed it
My righteous walk has borne all sin, so how then can I be righteous?
Never!
There's not one righteous; no, not one All have
sinned and fallen short of the Glory of God
Amen ...
It's God's righteousness that lives

So Necessary

Lord, I'm a little nauseous, spirit stirred up;
deliverance is on the forefront.
Holy Ghost … moving within me.
Infirmities lifted up … exiting, no longer a part of me.
My temple filled … my flesh, moving real still.
Jesus reign … on me.
Minister to my spirit, strengthen my bones.
Increase is needed, motivation has exceeded, desire is speaking.
Passion of the Christ.
An inspiration.
Not the movie but His life.
The truth, manifested.
My will, caresses the cross.
I hunger and thirst; don't want to be lost.
This walk is so necessary.
Persecution is a must; righteousness is needed.
It's so necessary.
O Lord, I push through the multitude in
remembrance of you because
IT'S SO
NECESSARY

Watching

As I fall into a stance of mourning,
not knowing whether I'm coming or going,
I feel lost, empty, but I know you are near, abiding close.
Hand stretched out, still beckoning, calling.
Opportunity at my reach; hard to accept it.

What's holding me back?
What stronghold is on attack?
No more binding; it's time to let loose!
Let me go!

I'm that eagle; soar high, live low.
I'm on a journey, fulfilling a mission, already predestined
and known to make it.
Failure is not an option.
Call it pride, but I will not lose!
The battle has been won.
By faith, I feel victories breathing.
Appearance defeated;
spiritually, I achieved it!
All through King Jesus!

Be Encouraged

For in the time of need, when we're faced with
storms brought on by life's equations,

we must always remember to trust God and pray.

We must lean not on our own understanding but seek Him.

He is the light to all dark hallways.

He's the best comforter when we're lacking inner security.

The best provider when "to improvise" can't even be considered.

His death proved it

when he took captivity captive and bared it all.

Unadulterated Truth

Heavenly Father,
God of all living and the dead,
defeated death; the grave couldn't hold him, rose in three days,
tearing down the middle wall of partition,
boldly before the throne of grace …
My time of need.

Praying without ceasing,
speaking the word of God,
releasing power,
breaking chains,
no longer bounded.

I AM FREE
from the hands of the enemy,
no longer under his control,
nor can I be influenced into Believing
and comprehending his lies.
The father of lies, since the beginning of time,
birthed deception in the garden of Eden,
perverted and molested from the beginning
with the mother of all living.

Robbed mankind of our innocence,
tainted our nature and were still seeking coverings…
hiding in church buildings,
relying on church positions,
refusing to become intimate
No engrafted
revelation word.

Neglecting the soul,
disregarding the love of the truth,
embracing delusions, believing the lies
of the enemy. The devil
pushing and peddling religion.
A veiled heart, blended and crowded in darkness,
rebuking, refusing light,
speaking ignorant of dignitaries
but claiming larger territories,
living unseasoned,
professing to be wise … fools.
God's people do not consider
turning completely to King Jesus
so the veil can be lifted.
Holy Scriptures living,
defiled by our own belief system.
Fleshly preaching,
misled in self-willingness, emotionally driven
intellectual beings holding zeal
but not according to God's righteousness.
Serving our own righteousness,
no submission to God's righteousness;
there is a difference.

No understanding of the Holy Scripture,
no deliverance,
only self-hindrances and intentions are evident.
A heart in the wrong position.

The word manifested
the true proverb confessing;
revealed in the New Testament.

The Kingdom

Due to the hindrances of the lust of my flesh that hinders,
it's my soul that surrenders
my will; delivered,
manifested in the Lord's mission.

The indwelling of the Holy Spirit is living
fruit of the spirit, giving.
People of God is… missing;
submitted to… religion.

Lust of the flesh, eyes, and pride of life… seeking big business.
The love of the world
neglects kingdom, seeking… disobedience.
Easily misled, the prince of the power of air… deceiving.
The love of the truth… not receiving.

The Holy Spirit is grieving.
Relationship, deep intimacy.
The manifestation of his power is only in his kingdom.
There is no defeated nor the gates of hell superseding!

Powers and principalities,
familiar, trampled on by
the Kingdom.

Remember the 7 Sons of Sceva?
The law has been fulfilled in King Jesus.

The #1 commandment under grace …
SEEK YE FIRST THE KINGDOM.

Fruits of the Spirit

There is a LOVE that empowers a deep-seated JOY.

Being FAITHFUL to God brings
OBEDIENCE for strength to endure

LONG-SUFFERING as PATIENCE

Establishes herself in SELF-CONTROL

And with these there is no law

Earthly Vessel

But by the Grace of God I am what I am.
I never said it but the Lord declared it.
She's more than a conqueror;
the apple of his eye
on the sparrow.

Fearfully and wonderfully made in the eye of the beholder,
He watches over me,
protects, guides me in all spiritual truth,
even the deeper things of God.

He's given me an unction of discernment,
through him I see
as I triumph over the public spectacle, the devil.
Christ defeated the grave, nailing all powers,
principalities to the cross.
Delivered me from all spiritual darkness;
no longer lost.

Christ reigns as the head of my life.
He gives more abundantly and he came that I might obtain it.

He gave that I might freely give.
He suffered at his own discretion;
doing the will of the father
through obedience, became the blessing.

A treasure in earthen vessels.

I Am …

I AM
not black.

But I AM called me out of darkness.
I AM
Dirty because of the sin I was born in.

My color, my race, does not determine who I AM.
My character is formed in God's image therefore I AM pure.

No spot, no blemish.

I know who
I AM …

Deserving

Living in the present
with the presence of God.
For the moment, the time being right now.

I focus.
I push.
I strive.

I live to give.
I give to live.
Fruits of the spirit, discerning.

Unworthy,
but God says
I'm deserving!

Creation

As the night falls, the stars are drawn even as the
rain chases the canvas ... we call land.

Spoke into existence, a move of God's hand
danced all across creation; created man
in his own image, breathed the breath of life in
our nostrils ... now we are a living soul.

Time goes on, God see our heart as "continual evil."
One man's sin made us all evil
as one man's death brought righteousness.
Now we stand as a body of believers.
Christ is the only way to eternal life.
If I believe, is there a need to change? Or can I
live in eternal life and remain the same?

As I sit back, judge others, harbor unforgivingness, love to gossip;
backbiting is my hobby and my "good deeds" say "I'm holy."
I'm a faithful tither but everyone knows me as a liar.
I'm eager to manipulate, smile as I deceive.
Self-exaltation is my religion.
I use seduction to apply the pressure to fulfill my ungodly pleasures.

I'm double minded: voicing I'm a Christian, living like I'm a sinner.
Don't be offended! Let's get it together.
Be honest to God, go through and get our deliverance.
Stop pretending; our actions are evident
that these spirits are prevalent.

Is our living for Christ in vain? Did he not raise from
the grave? Why then are we living as slaves?
Quoting scriptures, living only as believers
with a form of godliness but denying the power to be free.

More Than a Conqueror

I've built my house upon a rock and that rock is Jesus Christ.
Adversity encompassed me, injustice persecuted me, calamity
fell upon me but my faith in God didn't fail me.

It was my trust in God that held me together
as I trampled on the enemy, the adversary.
Through Christ I triumph over the open spectacle, the devil.
I'm more than a conqueror.
I'm more than a conqueror.

Trials and tribulations come to make me
strong—they can't break me!
So-called friends gone! Good, they don't make me!
A loss of material things don't shake me because every
word that proceeds from the mouth of God made me!
And I am who I am!
I'm more than a conqueror.
I'm more than a conqueror.

I've received the kingdom which can't be shaken;
therefore, no demonic force can break in.
I'm more than a conqueror.
I'm more than a conqueror.
Who wants to come up against me? God's chosen.
Who wants to try me? Favor all on me, God's anointed.

Even at your attempt, who then can be against me?
My God is not slack in any of his promises.
Not a man he should lie, not the son he should repent.
You uncircumcised Philistine
still trying to violate the army of the Lord.
If he spoke it, it exists.
Kingdom suffers violence, and the violent take it by force!

I'm more than a conqueror.
I'm more than a conqueror.

Jesus Reigns

Most precious father, God of all living and the dead,

as you live in the death of my flesh that can't submit,

my desire has risen as my eyes channel on hills
even as your will pants within me.

I'm familiar with it;
lined up with it.
Faith not wavering in it.

Received a kingdom, can't be shaken in it.

Fortified city, truly a believer, gates of hell can't prevail against it.

I AM VICTORIOUS.

Snake and scorpion trampler, more than a conqueror.

Soaring like an eagle, living like an eagle,
filthy rich in spirit, can't be defeated.
My God isn't slack.

The grave couldn't hold him; death never affected him.

JESUS CHRIST REIGNS.

Never leaving, never forsaking, is that bread
of life that rained down from heaven

The blessing poured out from the window of heaven.

The treasure in earthen vessels
supplying the need
became the foundation for a wayward perverse generation
just to raise up a Joshua generation.

Full of faith ... unafraid ... not ashamed ...
not guilty ... can't be blamed.

A desire to stand bold ... moving only in
obedience ... waiting, only to listen.

Just to follow the mission
as the battle is being won!

Jesus Christ Reigns

Good

My ... my ... my ...

My Father, my God, my Teacher, my only reason:
Jesus,
Minister.

The sole provider of any need,
the breath of fresh air we breathe.

Smooth, crisp, and clean,
beautiful clouds, dust from his feet.

Creator of all things,
spoken into existence.

His voice walks in the cool of the day,
heavy winds calm as he speaks;
ruler of all things.

A thought—it's done.
A word—it's already been written.

My Father, my God, my Teacher, my only reason—

Jesus.

Endurance

Perseverance reserves my place in the race.
The face of God is my passion.
Eyes on hills never witnessed the battle,
sweatless victory more than a conqueror.
Who needs a champion?

Love

Son Light

I love the SON when he shines upon me,
glowing
with a love complexion.

His embrace smothers me with affection,
sometimes we cuddle.

As he opens me up to dreams and visions,
He is the way, I follow the mission.

The Light

Father God, your word is my covenant with you.
Your light persuades me to abide in you.
Your stripes guide me.

My lust continuously tries me.
Obedience to what's inside me
wipes the tears As I am dying,
decreasing as the Holy Spirit increases.

Constantly reminding me …
I am the light of the world.
Satan,
get thee behind me!

Lover

When you tell me "I love you,"
I hear sweet love tunes.

When I look into your eyes,
I see the cries of hurt from your past life.

When I hold you in my arms
I feel your spirit rise, happily.

All knowledge that Jesus wipes the tears from your eyes ... always.

Guidance

Gracious Father handed over to me, a sinner unworthy but
bound by love everlasting. He is so precious,
wonderfully fashioned, a good Master,
strong Shepherd, thought about me, left me covered.
Sins blotted out, gone in the sea of forgetfulness.
Rebirthed in baptism, born again.
I see the light.
His stripes are my path as I walk in the spirit.

My King

My warrior, my protector, He's a God lover.

I respect Him; He's my hero; swept me off my feet.
He walks in confidence, rooted in strength; He is so strong.
He is not intimidated by my strength, on
the contrary, He encourages it!

Together, we are one: my body is his and vice-versa.
I love to rest in his arms.
His embrace shields me from harm.
He is my king
and I'm forever loving him.
With the love of Christ,
He loves me unconditionally.
He is my king and I'm not concerned about anything!
My king got it!
He handles it all!
As I stand, right there, engrafted in his side,
I'm not going anywhere.
He lacks, I give unto him.
When he wax weak, I speak encouragement.
I sing a song of sweet lullabies spoken into our being.
Then he smiles at the attraction.
Of the revelation that
I am his queen and I know my king.

What about Me?

I dwell in the midst of a being.
Bones and tissues surround me.
I'm covered in flesh.
A flesh that's recognized, where no good thing dwells.

What about me?
I'm the one that holds the strength, the breath in your nostrils.
I'm that light that shines in darkness.

I'm your inner being.
known before the foundation of the world,
way before color was considered.

What about me?
I made you.
Remember the storms?
Who carried you through?
Remember the pain when it was released from your eyes?
I'm that comforter, right there every time.

I shed the only color.
Where is that recognition?
Sundays, Easter, and Christmas. It all sounds like tradition.

I'm the one that has got you where you are today.
Without any recognition; grace, mercy, and love abiding.
Still, I am your Father, your only provider.

Love

Father God, I love you.
Love is powerful,
so powerful it changes, rearranges the mind-set.

It establishes a strong standard when believing in it.
Love is beautiful.
It covers a multitude of sins, closer than the next of kin.

Love is strong, it keeps me fighting all day long
just to accomplish it in life, to have, to hold.
In submission to shape, break, mold.
Love cleanses, it purifies
the depth of the soul.

Love is an inspiration, a desire for me to be just like it.
I just love to love.

Never really experienced it physically
but spiritually. I've sacrificed
only to get to know it.
Made obedience much easier, ended up being well pleasing.

The apple of someone's eye that watches over me, cares for me.
Every single hair on my head accounted for.
Loves me, never forsaken, never leaving
abiding, comforts me when I am crying
And when I believe a lie,
he chastises me
only because of love
that died for me ...
LOVE,
LOVE,
LOVE.

Filled

Lord, I stand within your midst,
a willing, able vessel
for filling my due bill, filled
cup running over,
voice spoken, tongue swollen, utterance
sounds of another language,
spirit taken over, communicating
my prayer language.

Holy Ghost abiding.
I in him, him in me.
Love feelings run from my eyes.

Righteousness is on the rise.
Peace is in my mind.
My God, followed through
right on Time!

I'm not worthy but Almighty loves me anyway.
I'm not worthy but he blessed me.
In my mess he loves me
and I'm not worthy of this blessing.
Holy Spirit loves me.

Lost Love?

Talk to me love.
Love where are you?
I need you love.
Love don't leave me.
Love,
Love, can you hear me?
It's you, love, that places a smile
upon my face.
I need you;
can't continue without you.

Love, you motivate me;
inspire me to be an inspiration to those
who don't know you,
desire you, even those who
abuse you, use you,
despise the very action of you
because they are confused by you.

Love, all their lives been
accused righteously, judged, and
rebuked for neglecting you.
Love, where are you??
I've lost you.
I'm looking for you.
Love,
don't leave me.

Grown Man

A man leaves his mother and father
to cling to his wife.
The two become one flesh.

HE IS A GROWN MAN!
Boys stay home!
Grown man come get me, cling to me
Be my head as Christ remains your head.
God Almighty, in full reign,
this bed, undefiled.
resting in the comfort of the Holy Spirit.
The power of God
protecting in love,
unity manifested.

Marriage!

I'm so in love, my heart is rent.
Bowed down before the king.
Submitted to my king, this is easy.
Well pleasing joy overwhelmed, heart skips a beat
and still I exhale.

Love is in the air.
In his absence, I still feel his presence.
His scent lingers in every single room of our home.
The King of the castle,
he knows what he owns; nobody can tell him differently.

He stands strong in adversity
when encompassed by the wicked,
Never moved by circumstances.

He is a grown man and I love him
as I stand to encourage him.
Prayers, supplications offered up.
Power of the Holy Spirit before him,
Even his confidence, who owns him?
A place of maturity!
Child-like actions are no longer a reaction.

He is a grown man!
And I'm happily in love with him.
Don't mind doing what he asks of me.
His expectations of a woman, I hold them
even as I hold my tongue to speak those things that are edifying.

A Strong Woman Has Arisen

The strong woman has arisen,
made from old pain—tears,
many and plenty of disappointments that
brought on fear.

Embracing low self-esteem, empty inside,
my strength is weak but I still don't cry.
My belly is tensed,
nauseous, can't eat.
Wondering why—who am I? Really?
Seeking for answers, I turn to the Holy Spirit.

The determination to feel love is what I
was missing, not religion.
On the contrary, intimacy with God—
that's why I exist.

The strong woman is getting strength
spiritually, my God took the pain, wiped the tears,
made my disappointments a drive for success.
I belong to him.
I own confidence; I'm no longer shy.
I talk about him. I love him.
Jesus, I love you.
And I thank you for dealing with my self-esteem issues.
Now, when I cry, I cry tears of joy
because I am loved.
THE STRONG WOMAN HAS ARISEN.

Relationship

A Force To Be Reckoned With ...

I come submitted to obedience in Christ Jesus.
All power and authority moving mightily with me.

Trampling on snakes and scorpions, wiles of the devil
an open spectacle.
I triumph over the enemy, defeated,
stripped of all powers and principalities,
nailed to the cross.

A force to be reckoned with ...

No more condemnation.
All are born in, shaped in,
Created equal,
same opportunities:
redemption, reconciliation, deliverance,
same self-hindrances, same evil hearts continuously.
I seek God's face religiously.
Heart bowed before the King, consistently.

A force to be reckoned with ...
Only in King Jesus
where I stand firm
as he is lifted up,
drawing all men.

Encouraged Deliverance

It's been a long time since I've spoken to you
in poetry format.

So I decided to reach back and do that.
From a different light in renewed understanding,
I stand to encourage.

Not you but your relationship in King Jesus.
Even as it grows to intimacy,
that's the "baby" conceived in your womb …
beautiful.

I'm talking about the deliverance of the enlightenment
of your God-given life.

This is passion in action.
Reaction to every fraction that tried to
break you, accuse you, mislabel you.

But the love of God took all the abuse for you.
Now you can be free,
stand unashamed,
guilt-free
and well-deserving.

Spiritual Warfare

Although I thought I was standing,
I neglected to heed understanding
of the Holy Scriptures.

I stumbled into a fall where my feelings and
emotions put a crack in this wall.
This fortified city is under attack!
Feelings and emotions took my focus,
lost sight on discernment, hopeless
tricks, schemes, wiles of the devil—the culprit!

But glory be to God,
I'm not ignorant of his devices
nor my own lust and enticements.
That I'm tired of fighting;
I'm tired of going through.

Facing weariness in well doing,
multiple cases of depression,
soul waxed with vexation,
one single persecution of loneliness,
emptiness, false feelings of despair.

SPIRITUAL WARFARE!
The devil is a liar!
The spirit of God is abiding.

His kingdom is established.
Inherited.
No means of shaking it; can't be moved!
Uprooting mountains,
breaking chains,
faith not wavering,
stepping out of the grave.

Headed towards salvation's door,
grave clothes,
cover the floor!

Abba Father

I stand before you, in awe of you due to your calling,
Abba Father.
Delivered, cleansed, set free, an unmovable Kingdom within me,
can't be shaken, gates of hell can't prevail against me.
A fortified city consumed by the indwelling of the Holy Spirit,
watchmen on the wall, even as a fence of angels protect me.
There is no going to and fro in me,
the weapon to seek and devour has been destroyed;
no longer against me.
A tree planted by the rivers of water
birthing fruit in my season,
Abba Father.
Extended grace,
didn't take it in vain
but waited as I pressed toward the mark.
Eyes on hills, neglected weariness while doing good,
submitted to the King, mounted up with wings,
endured long-suffering as I searched out those things, which remain
where Christ is seated on the right hand of God,
where grace and mercy reside.

Abba Father,
I cry tears of joy from the overwhelming
of your illuminating presence.
Abba Father,

I forever offer up the sacrifice of praise, fruit of my lips;
the aroma brings forth your habitation that I yearn for.
A strong manifestation to be conformed to.
That image released in man's nostrils
as I stand in the midst of it;
girded up in it
on my face
as I worship it.
The unadulterated word of truth,
Abba Father,
I bear witness of it.

Spiritual Connection

Lord, my spirit sings to you sweet love songs
and beautiful tunes of "I love you."

Lord, my spirit cries from the inside, crowded
where it resides too much stuff.

Lord, my spirit waits for the anointed
word, the fire that wakes me up.

Lord, this is me, your spirit, patiently standing
by, communicating with you
while my flesh sleeps.

Relationship

This blood was shed.
A death bed was filled.
Power was given.
Life was resurrected.
A walk became a stance.

Word was spoken, witnesses were fed.
Different steps were ordered, faith increased.
Believers walked with hope while selves decreased.

Life was given.
The light is the reason minds become renewed.
Spirituality is all that was needed.
A connection conceiving the best, everlasting;
forever lasting
relationship,
eagerly breathing.

Strength

I stand as a damsel built on God's strength.
Skin baked to a beautiful shine.
I'm so fearfully and wonderfully made.
I came from heartache and pain.
My tears formed my footstool.
My rainy days soothes the bruises in my
body and moistens my hands.
My body is strong, made from anointed bones.

I'm prone to caress obedience.
I walk in confidence, shaped in righteousness.

My steps are ordered in God's will.
I remain covered in the blood.
My wrongs blotted out, thrown in the sea of forgetfulness.
His sheep, I am,
holy, acceptable
God is phenomenal and I am phenomenally-created in his image.
No spot.
No blemish.

Rest

Heavenly, precious Father,

My Lord, his life.
I fall back as the Holy Spirit springs forth.
Take control in dwelling
All over me.
Intimately,
He knows me, I am his passion.
He chose me
and he holds me.
Wrapped in his arms, safely kept.
Head on his bosom …
entered that rest.

Life Speaks

O how beautiful, how I adore you.

Majesty, royalty, righteousness.

Holy, holy, holy,
you are never affiliated with sin,
stink in your nostrils.

You're better than good; awesome is not enough.
Words can't begin to explain the simple things in regards to you.
The mind can't begin to contemplate the wisdom you hold.
Communication is limited due to the fact that
the description of words are not enough.
Expression, so I say nothing.
But I remain submitted as my peculiar walk talks to this generation.
The spirit of truth speaks as
folks embrace salvation.

My Covenant

I made a covenant with mine eyes—focused, always on the Lord.

I made a covenant with my mouth to always
speak God's word, the truth.

I made a covenant with my mind—to always
meditate, open to be renewed.

I made a covenant with my feet—to always follow
my shepherd because I am his sheep.

I made a covenant with my God—If I always look with His eyes,
speak His words, think spiritually, and always go where He leads.

If I do these things, would He …
Give me a heart transplant and make me clean?

It Is Finished

Lord God,
as I stand, even as I follow,
you are my guide.
I abide in you.
Your comfort protects me
and your spirit enlightens me with understanding.

I'm grateful, forever thankful, for your love that covers me,
smothered my sin, allowed me to be a friend,
engrafted me in as a partaker of your heavenly calling.
Faith not wavering, received the kingdom,
can't be shaken, victory embraces her!
God's presence changed her.

The word became her
because obedience made her more than a
conqueror. Snake and scorpion trampler,
a mercy pleader, a grace receiver,
obtainer,
went to the king boldly before the throne,
my time of need.

Yolk destroying anointed power,
no longer bounded.
Mountains no longer "thinking", climbing
but "speaking". The word
from a foundation of power
that uproots, breaks chains,
and tears down every single stronghold.
NOW
I fight from victory.
The battle of the mind has been won.
It is written, it is finished.
So it is done!

Triumphal Entry

It's a triumphal entry—
a garment of praise.
Righteousness tore down the stage and established the way.

It's a triumphal entry—
Waving holy hands.
Hosanna! Hosanna! Hosanna!
Riding in on this babe.

It's a triumphal entry—
I am victorious through Christ Jesus!
I trample over every single one of my enemies.
A public spectacle.

Delivered from the powers of darkness,
Raised; walking in the newness of life.
I seek those things which are above,
Where Christ is seated.

Obedience is fulfilled.
Every imagination, thought, demonic stronghold—
The Lord rebuke you!
The Lord rebuke you!
And I offer up this sacrifice of
PRAISE!

Lord Jesus

As I keep mine eyes on the hills, I focus on my life.
Your passion burns with desire.
Your will sparks a fire within me.

I can't go astray.
My anchor of hope that keeps me afloat,
the chief cornerstone,
maker of this building,
a fortified city,
can't be condemned.

Father God,
your word is my covenant with you.
Your light persuades me to abide in you.
Your stripes guide me.

My lust continuously tries me;
obedience to what's inside me,
wipes the tears
as I am crying.

Decreasing as the Holy Spirit increases;
constantly reminding me
I am the light of the world.
Satan, get thee behind me!

My Father God

My Father God,
my high tower that provides every hour
everything I need. My treasure,
abiding in this earthly vessel.
A story constantly being told,
a never changing message unfolds.

Revelation behind the veil,
boldly before the throne I travail.
Traveled the way Jesus prevailed.

Intimate Relationship

Father God, it's time to separate from all false
religious belief systems and establish
relationship
where you have called us
in deep intimacy,
communion in the spirit,
abiding in your presence, standing in awe of you,
feeling heaven.

Eyes cast upon your Glory of light.
It's your illuminating presence that gives
definition to this broken, contrite soul.

I'm forever repentant.

Labelled, woe is me.

Born, already against you.

Raised to hate change.

Embrace shame,
point blame,
never truly understanding the importance of
responsibility but always professing innocence.

As guilt offered me coverings,
pride introduced a new attitude that abandoned truth
even as it stole my identity as I ran.

Denied your image in which I was created,
a way of acceptance,
a degree in freedom
revealed death.

As I now live in
the Garden of Eden.

I'm Solid

As I stand on solid ground, the rock,
I can't be moved.
Trials and tribulations don't shake me,
Hard times made me.

I'm like a city that's fortified,
A pillar that withstands a storm.
The anchor that keeps me afloat, only to hold on.

I shall not lose.

I'm built from solid ground.
I'm that rose, sprouted from concrete.
Nothing can stop me.
I drive motivation as I reside in determination.

Jealousy and folks hating, ammunition for me to make it.

Ducking and dodging every blow from the opposition,
Call me victory in remission.

The teacher that gives permission,
The judge that upholds the law,
The sign that gives the lost direction,
The motherless affection, the fatherless protection.
I AM SOLID.

I stand on solid ground.
I step with a solid stance.

I speak from a solid foundation of truth
known to correct and rebuke.

I will not lose.

I'm solid.
Call me thirty-eight hot, sweating bullets … 100 proof,
Strong from within, that's why I can't be broken.

I'm solid from the inside out, nothing can stop me!

Oppression has left me.
Depression has detested me.
Suppression alleviated me
While solitude became intimate with me,
Deposited seed within me,
conceived in me,
then held me.

In solitary confinement
until I could get past the crying
as the tears replenished and strengthened me
to withstand every trick, scheme, and scam of the enemy's hand.

IM SOLID!

Good Fight of Faith

Messiah,

I'm tired of crying; fighting
opposition is always against me. Before me
a host of demonic forces target me,
scrutinize me, plot and plan to lay attack on me
with hopes of faith wavering.
Ungodly thoughts of considering, tempting
due to the lust within me.

Messiah,
deliver me.

Window of escape, come get me.
Window of heaven, release, pour your Holy Spirit upon me.
Walk with me, saturate me … fill me with your Holy Spirit.

Operate in every single gift of your spirit.
My soul desires you,
stands in agreement with you,
in purpose from you.

I pursue you, seek you
in fellowship, communion.

As I walk in the cool of the day, being intimate with you,
feeling safe with you,
protected by you.

LOVE, surrounds me.
Joy strengthens me.
Peace soothes me; self-control remains still in me.
Gentleness brings serenity and goodness
during these times of long-suffering.

ON MY KNEES BEFORE YOU.
HEAD BOWED DOWN BEFORE YOU.
HEART RENT BEFORE YOU.

Tears of replenishing builds, adds virtue in me.

Mustard seed of faith produces growth in me.

So I stand in the midst of the storm,
knowing the battle has been won.
As I go through the fiery furnace,
purging me of all infirmities,
coming out!
PURE as GOLD.

Voice

Father God, as I stand before you,
held accountable to you,
your word, fire, shot up in my bones;
will not keep quiet.

The truth, I stand behind it.
Emotions, feelings, I deny them.
Led by your spirit, the word my guidance.

Opinions, fleshly understanding, I undermined them,
deny them. Dare not to consider nor try them.

The good Shepherd.

This sheep hears your voice, the true teachings and another

I will not listen!

The Good Shepherd

Lord, I've picked up my cross, it's heavy.
Teach me to walk steady.

That old man is buried.
I want to be holy,
dressed in your righteous clothing.
Your bride, joined in holy matrimony.

Enlarge our territory.
Let your will be done.
I am your glory,
sending forth praises.

Thankful for the Alpha, grateful for the Omega.

This is my story.
Jesus is my future.
Words of my mouth, meditation of my heart,
acceptable in his sight.

My Lord, my light.
My breath, his life.
My body, his temple.
My steps, his walk.
My voice, his talk.
My desires, his will.
My land, his mighty hand.

Obedience

You don't know what's inside of me.

You don't know what God has told me.

You don't know what's been revealed to me.

You don't know.

You don't know.

I'm the last, considered the least, but

I'm that Mary that sat at his feet,

Listened, reverenced his speech

instead of running around prepping and preparing a feast.

I'm that baby,
babe in Christ, that the mother, the saints
rolled over and took its life.

That's why I am the one

who can stand still and encourage myself in the Lord.

You don't know what's inside of me.

You don't know what God has told me.

You don't know what's been revealed to me.

You don't know.

You don't know.

Thoughts of You

As I sit here, thoughts of you surface, captivate my mind.
I'm focused,
Eyes on you even as I miss you.
My desire unfolds, my lack stands bold.
Inhabited by your presence,
A place of comfort,
An embracement of love,
A peace with no understanding.
I can't even explain it!

The feeling is overwhelming.
I rest my head close to your bosom.
The beloved disciple
On display in the bond of unity and love
Built me up.
My anchor of hope keeps me afloat.
My strong tower holds me up.

In the toughest hour,
My chief cornerstone
Resides, still
As my
Father.

Thankful

Victory

I lift up my hands,
Holy, acceptable.
O Lord, are they pleasing in your sight?
To move within your might?

Casting, healing, rebuking in your mighty name.
This is warfare!

She is more than a conqueror.
A Satan-rebuker,
Snake and scorpion trampler.

Dominion ruler,
Captivity leader,
Fortified city …
Victory breathing.

Love Letter to Christ

I miss you, our time we spent together.
Your love, there is no other
Agape, unconditional,
no respect of persons.

This love has chosen a seed that can breed
and grow into a beautiful tree
rooted in living water, strengthened by the strong tower,
built by the master builder.

Protected, a fortified city
but free.
All walls of Jericho
fall down!
Mounted up with wings that soar,
leading me to another place
in love with a different face.

Feeling his passion of love for his own special creation,
wrapped in his embrace,
moving in his patience, never anxious.

Prayers, supplications,
requests made
standing still.

Strong Tower

Precious Father, I bow my heart unto thee.

Opened, ready to be renewed in you.

Change.

It needs to happen, a manifestation of your presence,

A desire of my habitation.

Your will is my only mission.

Obedience is my submission.

Your grace and mercy,

In remembrance.

The armor of God keeps me in deliverance.

Anchor of hope

Keeps me afloat.

The lily in the valley,

The rose of Sharon,

My prince of peace,

Breath and bread of life,

The lion and the lamb.

King of kings.

THE GREAT I AM!

Strong Woman

As a woman standing strong,
Firm backbone, prone to success,
God predestined this vessel of desire.

She's chosen to be his daughter.
A little bit peculiar, walking in her Father's image,
Broken from all spots and blemishes.

Look at his baby girl.
A holy nation on the rise, sin is despised.
Righteousness right before your eyes.

Look at her stepping in royalty.
She's beautiful from within.
Where the spirit resides as her guide,
She's a sanctuary
Standing strong,
firm backbone.

If My People

The sounds of the world, I hear.
The noise surrounds me.
Hollering, cursing, fussing, souls thirsting.
Negativity, hard times, poverty cries,
Unrighteousness is birthing.

A world where equality resides only when it's beneficial.
A place where what's right is wrong.
So how can one tell the difference?

To live by faith?
Hoping, evidence of things not seen
Yeah right
But claim we still believe.

In God I trust
That he will still love me;
Be there for me in my wrong,
Engaging in my beliefs That the heart is right
Even though my actions are wrong.

I Am a Queen

Strong woman of God, all enemies defeated. I've been there, in the pits.

Searching for light in the darkness.

I've traveled through deserts where the sun dimmed its light.

Cooled the heat and ordered the water to come quench me.

And I have yet to be thirsty.

I am a queen and you can't help but to love me.
I've lived a hard life, formed from concrete.
I am the rose that ignorance can't see.
That's why there are rose petals subjected at my feet.

I am a queen. I'm fearfully and wonderfully made beautiful, inside where it counts.
I'm glowing, mind-blowing, searching just to see what I'm about.
My heritage is royalty that's why I'm always going to shine.

Never in anyone's range, prosperous. Never going without, blessed.
I walk and nothing but good comes to me.
When I run, nothing but the best chases me. And when I'm relaxed, motivation and success make love to me.
I AM A QUEEN!

89

Grace

Eyes on the prize and the hills,
God's will,
He is faithful, never forsaking.

Begging bread?
Not his chosen.

Love covers a multitude,
Even a generation of God haters and religious debaters.

God's choice made us his chosen.
For it is written.
It is finished.
It is over.

The Lamb's Book

My gracious Father, it's your diligence that inspires me,
Your passion that drives me.
Your strength I abide in.
Your joy that continuously allows me to do,
to remain faithful and embrace "Mrs. Patience"
as I humble my heart, bringing obedience back into submission.

LOVE
has brought me home.
I can't live without it.
Death has crowded me, took the life up,
up out of me.
Estranged wife?
No, the devil keeps lying to me.
He keeps trying me, deceiving me,
attempting to mislead me
but I'm covered in the blood of
KING JESUS!
I can't reason with him
because it's the Holy Scriptures that keep me breathing.
I'm not claiming to be a vessel of honor
but a vessel of threat!

To the powers and the principalities in the heavenlies,
and because of the Kingdom of God that is embedded in me …
They have every single reason to be scared of me.

Through the Power of God, I trample over the enemy.
His host and entourage
second guess and scrutinize plans when coming near me
as I walk in the spirit,
shunning the lust of the flesh eye and pride of life.

Latoera Denise O'Neal
Written
in the Lamb's Book of Life.

Trust God

As the race thickens, the storm rages.
The current is stronger, my strength weakens.
God's strength is stronger.
Endurance is the key that unlocks everything unto me.

To continue to go on as I go on to continue,
carry me O Lord, comfort me in my distress, deliver me from my
mess.

I confess my sin. I must die so I can live.
This journey is a continuous stance, can't be shaken.
Dry bones have been awakened.
The word has been spoken,
stirring up the anointing.

I'm healed, no more hurting!
The pain is gone.
The cleansing is in process, holiness manifested,
righteousness confessing!

Healed

Lord, I look to you, for and in all things—HEALING.

Of my heart, past hurts
that enabled me to find comfort in lies
as I denied,
opened the door for the enemy to kill and destroy
every single opportunity of life he took from me.
The desire of love
when he abused, took advantage,
misused me
in his perverse ways.
He used. And older, young,
broken man, bound in sexual urges
to defile me,
molest me.
NOW, I trust no man.

Confused in my sexuality
placed me with a lost identity,
dressed me in characteristics of that same broken man.

That as I grew up, I couldn't stand.
I'm lost in sin that I was born in
the world.

But I refuse to live and comfort any sin of the heart.
UNFORGIVINGNESS,
I must move on

Lord, I look to you for and in all things--HEALING.

Saturate me with your love as I give.
Replenish me with your loving kindness as I live.
Relinquish your strength to my inner man,
edifying the body,
restoring. Restoration to all creation.
Overcoming by the words of my testimony,
the blood of the Lamb.

Sweet Melodies

Holy Spirit,

Moving mightily within me, fill me.

Making sweet melodies in me, grab ahold, shake, break chains, unloosen strongholds.

All walls of Jericho need to fall down, be gone.

No longer holding me captive, locked down, imprisonment, prayed.

My God was listening, an aide to troubles; soothing balm in Gilead.

Comforter like no other, all time agape, lover.

Part-time, nothing.

Full-time everything, completely understanding.

Stronger than man.

My world developed in his hands.

Holy Spirit,

Move mightily within me,

Fill me, making sweet melodies in me.

Harmonize beautiful lullabies.

Harp playing, Spirit singing.

The sound of music is in my cry,

The notes,

Passing through my eyes.

Mouth opened, drums beating,

Inner being is speaking.

Is anyone listening?

The breath entered the nostrils,

Anointed the bones,

Baptized the soul,

Created a new heart,

Reversed my blood,

And gave me a new start.

Holy Spirit,

Moving mightily within me.

Fill me.

Make sweet melodies with me.

The Devil Is a Lie!

Some said I'll never amount to anything.
I tried so hard to prove them wrong.
My choices made them right.

Tried so hard not to be like my mother.
I ended up just like her.
I am her shadow.

Never knew my father; met him at twenty-six years old.
Realized, I am his image.
I'm just like him!
All resemblances are in the bones
Which can't be broken, holding all the anointing.

My blood is thirsty, the breath is circulating,
Misinterpreted as my oxygen.
The breath of life is my life,
Holy Ghost residing.
As I live mounted from spoken nothings!
As I live mounted from spoken nothings!
As I live mounted from spoken nothings!

My father heard them.
He knew I was hurting.
Revealed himself,
Began rebirthing.

Thank You

Holy God,
I hold on to you, your promises.
I am filled.
Thank you.
I confess my sins, righteously.
Before you,
I live
Holy, holy, holy.

Hands exalted before you.
Heart rent before you.
Mind renewed in you, things of you,
Pertaining to you, as I live.

Pressing towards the mark, faith increased,
Unbelief decreased.
The weight, the sin,
So easily beset me. Change has ran to the forefront a new creature
has been
Birthed.

Old things passed, I am new in action.
Vocabulary increasing to motivation.
Exceedingly above, all I can ask or think
Humbly,
I thank you.

Prayers

Ask

Father God,
rest in me, remain within me,
take not your spirit away from me.

There is a need ... supply,
come through like a winnowing fan,
breaking up hardened hearts,
granting a new start.
WE NEED OUR SAVIOR.

"FAITH"
has been our safe haven.

Increase in the things of God.
Shine your light in our hearts.
A vision is necessary.
Knowledge is mandatory.

Wake Up

At night when I close my eyes,
my tears rule my insides.
My pain, loaded up
my feelings, almost giving up
but my heart won't let me.

Life, hard times, and messed up situations

won't get me
down.
I'm at my lowest,
in God I trust.
Got to stay focused,
can't lose it when I'm already lost.
Swimming in my sins
as my soul pays the cost.

Lord, I need you.
I'm on fire, I'm burning internally.
No fallen tears,
they're held up because they are burning me.

My flesh is the leader, my lust is the boss.
My soul afflicted,
still paying the cost.

Lord, help me
break the mold.
My actions are itching. Quality time
I'm missing. My soul, crying out.

Sorrowful, sick, and afflicted.
Wounded.

The armor of God neglected,
no longer using it.

Help Me

Lord, help me.

I don't want to be in the midst of the weeping and the gnashing of the teeth.
I don't want to so see your back as you say "depart from me."
I know you not,
you worker of iniquity.

As a sinner, I stand strong for correction
because my choices lead me astray.
My actions placed me from under your protection.

Lord, help me. I need a Heavenly Father lesson.

Chastisement, don't want it but I know I need it.

Flesh, disobedient
spirit constantly feigning
for you, The word, the good news embedded in my heart.

My flesh, my spirit,
when will this battle stop?

Lord, help me.

Increase my faith.
I believe and if knowing is half the battle
and the battle is yours,
how then can I lose?

So I just pray, as a sinner with nothing to say
except "Lord, help me."

Have mercy
everyday.

Surrender

Lord,
I need your temple cleaned,
swept, no mess, no spot,
no, not even a blemish.

Pile that junk up,
purge it out of me.
The desires, the acts, the thoughts
that won't allow you to smile on me.

You know about them.
The judgmental judging,
the lascivious loving,
the gossiping, the smooth-talking, the hatred, the anger,
the feelings of those that despise,
the jealousy,
the physical fight that birthed death in my life.

Pile that junk up and purge it out of me.
The desires to freely drink strong drinks,
lusting after the material things that the world holds for me.

Lord, abide in me, make me clean.

An alternate cannot be considered.

I now, with no choice, I Surrender!

My Blessing

I'm a sinner, received salvation; saved by grace through faith.

I die daily, encompassed by the wicked. My own members, I take it personal.

Born in sin, shaped in iniquity through Christ, I have the victory!

This fight of faith is a lifetime battle, a journey considered a race.

Steps are ordered, patience required, faithfulness determines my hire.

I die daily.

I must obtain to achieve a place in this faith race called, turned, and still seeking.

The deeper the intimacy, the deeper the sin.

Woe is me!

A woman of unclean lips, thoughts, acts and heart.

Still dying daily.

Choosing not to give up,

Eyes lifted up,

Holy faith built up,

Garment of praise,

Dressed up, armor of God,

Girded up,

Verbal sacrifices offered up,

Window of heaven opened up,

Spirit of God lifted me up!

This is my blessing,

This is the place on earth as it is in heaven.

The presence, of God walks with me as I DIE DAILY.

This is my blessing.

Almighty Father

As I lay before you, opened up,
Vulnerable, ready for change,
My mind, renewed.
My heart, changed from a deeper root.

Let your heart's desire produce
from this vessel.

As I walk in your presence, strengthened
With truth, even as I stand
In the midst of the storm, been born again
From a corruptible seed to a life that's
Everlasting.

Now, I breathe.
I love a life that's predestined; manifested
In the cool of the day.
Constantly in communion,
Revealed in fellowship,
Intimacy has conceived. The bread of life
I now eat.

Window of heaven has opened.
Window of escape released grace.
Your mercy, I embrace.
Thankful.

Patient, long-suffering viewed me
As your passion moved me
To go through, to get
Through …
Just as I live.

Holy God

I stand, a voice of praise, Thanksgiving.
Intercessions presented before you.
Word not returning void.
Spoken from a foundation of Power,
Moved by demonstration of your Spirit,
Filled with your never-ending presence,
I surrender my all to you.
Your will in completion,
I give in.
No longer kicking against the pricks,
I will go.
You lead, I follow.
Your direction at your discretion,
A willing, able vessel.
Pour into me,
Pour out,
The well never runs out.
Water Baptism in the Spirit
Brings forth change in the mind, in the heart of your people.
Enlightenment increases,
Faith builds most
Holy faith.
Boldly before the throne of grace.
Our time of need.

Supplications

The War Inside Me

Lord, I know you see the fight,
the struggle going on within.
These worlds, these rumors of wars,
manifested inside me.

Jacob and Esau, bound in a tussle.
I'm crying.
A woman in travail,
ready to birth
but I'm scared to push.

Afraid of the outcome,
don't know what's going to happen or what I'm going to produce.
Esau running wild and loose.
Jacob, in the spirit under subjection.

Help me! Help me! Help me, Lord!
These rumors of wars are inside of me
and it's been written. So it's been said.
It must happen but will I live to see it pass?

This walk is killing me.
What's good to me is not a friend to me.
On the contrary, it's the enemy. By any means necessary,
trying to kill me.

Good to the eyesight, enticing; he got me. Now, I'm scared.
Trapped in this world, struggling in this fight,
the war
inside me.

Break Me!

I'm barely standing and I live at a standstill.
I hold back, tired of being hurt.
I felt everything you've not only said but done to me.
That's why I'm a mess.
No name but you can call me blessed.

In the background behind the scenes, so no one sees me
As my false witness protects me.
Y'all know her, grown to love her.
She bold, can hold her own but she all wrong!

Her nasty mouth, her disrespectful conduct, fruit of her evil heart.
I see her jealousy, her mountain of hatred and anger
Rooted from low self-esteem. No one encouraged her. No one loved
her
But always pulled from her inner strength
Then talked about her, drug her name in the dirt; but when in need
blessed would be the first.

She always gave, lived as a slave, subjected to bondage, and resided in
a cage, surrounded by evil. Where is love?
That's all I needed.

I looked,
Tried to find, no one was breeding it.
The "need" grieved me; made the desire leave me.

Jesus was spoken, I believed but never heeded.
No strength to trust him, convinced by my false witness to remain
hidden
to let her run the show.

She was so selfishly greedy, mindful of her benefits,
fulfilling opportunities just to get a shine.
Falsely, her intentions were somewhat correct but her heart was evil.
Her heart was evil.
So I had to call on whom I believed in.
KING JESUS,
deliver me from this false witness.
I'm subjected to Jezebel, the false prophetess.

Deliver me, O Lord.
I know who I am and to whom I belong.
Take not your spirit away from me.
BREAK ME! BREAK ME!
BREAK ME from this STRONGHOLD!

Supplication

Lord,
I miss you, my spirit is sick, crying out to you…
SLOWLY dying,
In need of a word from you.

I confess with my mouth.
I love you.
My heart in the midst,
It's my actions that are different.
Will my spirit ever make it to heaven?

Living in this mess
Known as the body sinning in the flesh

Where no good thing dwells and ungodly desires are held.
No wonder it's so hard to walk, and yet so easy to talk.

Quitting is easier
But my crying out is the breather.
But to know,
That's the teaser.

To know is to wait
Which shakes this walk.
The stress, the pressure
Of being tested and tempted,
Infirmities manifested but not quite lifted.

But

Gifted and chosen
Set aside, brought out from amongst them
And it's not even over.

The Omega but the Alpha, the beginning.

Baptized, spiritually fed, born again, raised from the dead
And still not walking in the anointing.
My actions acting out,
not quite showing it.

So I'm thankful for the residue,
These spiritual poems.
From him, for me, recited unto you.

And I'm confessing my troubles
So it's spoken.
No longer a stronghold.
The enemies token
Now, it's on the forefront, out in the open

Ready to be broken.

Shining

Lord, I stand strong in desire.
My spirit screams
sounds of crying.

Godly sorrow is my attire,
the truth has been told.

So it is written,
Holy Spirit manifested.

My God, blessing.
My voice, confessing.
My actions, redirected.

Be Ye Holy for I am holy.
Now, I'm spiritually glowing.

Old baggage, no longer toting,
Strongholds, chains
broken.

This is life. This is the truth.
Walking, the word straight devil stalking.

No weapon formed against me shall prosper.

I call on his name in the midnight hour.

Tossing and turning,
Agitated,
Heart crying,
Spiritually dying.

Jesus is the truth and the devil is still a liar.

These mountains, I'm still speaking.
With his grace and mercy,

I'm still shining.

Deliver Me

Lord,
Take not your spirit away from me
As I stand upright before thee
In your righteousness,
Judged by you.

I adore your presence; in awe of you,
Consume me with your blessings
Of the Spirit.
The ability to speak life into existence,
Walking in all authority to hold all
Dominion, everything is subjected
In a disarray scattered abroad.
As the kingdom of God
Stands at hand,
Repent, be baptized, born again,
Break chains, loosen strongholds.
Walls of Jericho
Fall down,
Coverings of shame fall from me,
Fear step aside,
Spirit of Rejection come out from me.
Holiness reside.

Judgmental judging,
Gossiping,
That lying tongue.
O Lord set a guard over me.
Backbiting, self-righteous attitude,
I spew you from my mouth.
Get behind me
Sexual desires, don't you dare try me.
I feel an urge, an unction from the Holy Spirit.
It's time to be ... delivered!

Intercessions

Lost?

God's chosen are thirsty,
Lost, living in a hungry state,
Ate the accursed bait.

Faith, trust, and love the enemy has taken.
Sit and settle, living a life of ungodly acceptance.

Stuck, no drive, no strength,
Not even to conjure up,
To stand up, let alone do what's right.

In the battle but can't fight.
Carnal weapons, yeah right!
Already defeated.

The eyes' vision, prey on the opportunity of lust.
The vision of the heart, wicked, weak, and faint—who would trust?

The mind, lost, darkened, with no understanding.
The wool has covered their eyes, blinded.
The veil remains on the heart.

The SAVIOR is needed. The walking dead is at an increased rate.

God's chosen are thirsty, lost,
Living in a hungry state.

Intercession for Papa Smurf

Most heavenly precious Holy Father,
I stand before you upon my knees
focused on things above.
Mouth opened,
prayers and supplications,
heart submitted, open before you,
ready for change.

I've tried, I've tried, I've tried.
Nothing is working; my way has broken me to nothing.
That's why I now stand before you, another prodigal child.
Finished with wasteful living, my ears are listening
and my eyes need another vision!
I'm tired of feeling defeated, I'm tired of making choices that leave
me hopeless, and I'm tired of faking, relying on material things to be
thankful.
I need more.

I need something stronger. I need everlasting life
that provides, that overcomes. I want to become more than a
conqueror.
I want my life from within to begin, for I know I was predestined for
greatness.

Where do I start? How do I begin? Can you teach me? Can I be your
friend?
Will you look past my faults and tend to the need
of me needing my savior? Will you wink upon my mindless behavior?
Will you take away my mischanneled anger?

Can you help me to forgive those who hurt me, disappointed me, didn't encourage me
but talked about my bad choices? Condemned me in my errors
when they never lived in correction?

Yes, I consented to my own lusts but I never noticed anything better.
I tried to do right but lost that fight.
Now I see the battle is within me, even my wrong choices.
I've wronged you only and now I desire to make it right. Surely, this battle isn't over.
This weight I give to you to place on your shoulder
as I stand before you, without strength.
As my weakness becomes your strength.

Create in me a new person, place me in right standing.
I thank you for grace which you so graciously handed.
And your blood
which was shed
that I'm now covered in.

Intercessor

I sleep,

Dreaming about the truth.

I lay in the word,

I toss and turn in the pages.

I wake up praying.

Strengthen the Fathers

My Father of Fathers, turn the hearts of the fathers to the children.
This change is needed, abandonment is breeding.
A father goes on, leaving his child alone.
No care in the world because
the Love of the world.
A man's child is dreaming BIG DREAMS.
A DESIRE IS UNFOLDING to do something, to be someone.
This child laughs in confidence,
his drive says—I WILL MAKE IT!

He grows, even in age.
He looks and identifies lack.
No man to teach, no father to reach.
A drive no one encourages, it dies.

His dreams are buried.
Self-esteem, motivation are scared away.
Fear has resided,
feelings of no self-worth.

His voice as a grown man speaks—I CAN'T MAKE IT!

So I will live a lie and do what's not right
but I will be a better father than my old man!
Now he is self-righteous,

Led in deception, deceived by his own heart.
Established his own law,
no submission to the righteous law.

The gods of this age has darkened his eyes.
NOW HE IS LOST!
AND again,
A Father goes on leaving his child alone.
No care in the world because
the love of the world.
And another child is left
DREAMING!

Intercession

Gracious father,
I cry loud and spare not.
I lay prostrate
Before your grace.
Upon my face,
Your heart cries,
Released from my eyes.

Prayers, supplications, intercessions
On the rise
Elevated in your ears.
The will of your heart
Fluctuates.
Laborers are few, harvest is plenty.
We are
Oblivious.
Quenching the Spirit, unaware we're
Grieving you.

Lost on the power of the Holy Spirit,
Pharisees, Sadducees, Scribes
Reading the Scriptures.
Looking for King Jesus,
Neglecting to check inside;
Examine oneself
According to the Word of God.
Man can't judge us.

If we're Spiritual,
Spiritually discerned,
Operating under the anointing,
Destroying the yolk
Of bondage.
Gracious Father,
Purge us.
Fiery furnace burn us
As gold,
Releasing all infinities.
No longer robbing you.
Spiritual sacrifices,
Fruit of our lips,
A Spiritual
House for you
Laid out prostate
Before you.

Word of Truth

We have to hold on
In the faith of Jesus Christ.
A belief system that produces life
Everlasting.
No doubt not wavering,
Remain diligent in the race.
The swift can't withstand
The process of the building up
Of the most holy faith.
Our shield of Protection
From the world's affliction,
The gods of this age,
Strategic mission.

Saints of God,
We must hold on, remaining strong
In the bond of unity and love.
Helmet of salvation, mind renewed,
Seeking those things above.
Breastplate of righteousness
Upright before the King,
Held together with truth
Sharper than a two-edged sword
Rightly dividing
Our soul and spirit.

CPSIA information can be obtained
at www.ICGtesting.com
Printed in the USA
BVOW09s2127070817
491374BV00004B/23/P